EXPECTING AND EXECUTING

Balancing Career and Pregnancy

ADITI AGRAWAL

BlueRose ONE.com
Stories Matter
NewDelhi • London

BLUEROSE PUBLISHERS
India | U.K.

BlueRose ONE
Stories Matter
NewDelhi • London

For permissions requests or inquiries regarding this publication, please contact:

BLUEROSE PUBLISHERS
www.BlueRoseONE.com
info@bluerosepublishers.com
+91 8882 898 898
+4407342408967

ISBN: 978-93-6783-162-5

Cover design: Shubham
Typesetting: Sagar

First Edition: January 2025

Preface

Motherhood a word that holds a world of emotions, responsibilities, and transformation. For me, it's been a journey filled with unexpected turns, moments of clarity, and an ever-evolving understanding of what it means to "have it all." But here's the twist: I'm also a software developer. Balancing the demands of coding, problem-solving, and meeting deadlines with the unpredictable joys and challenges of motherhood has been a journey of contrasts. Each day brings its own obstacles, yet also moments of fulfillment that continue to surprise and inspire me.

This isn't a book about perfection. It's not about having all the answers or offering a one-size-fits-all guide. It's about the raw, unfiltered reality of trying to excel at work while embracing the messy, unpredictable beauty of motherhood. It's about the nights when you feel like you're failing at everything, and the mornings when you realize you're stronger than you thought. This book is a collection of my experiences, thoughts, and lessons a heartfelt attempt to offer insight and encouragement to anyone balancing motherhood and a demanding career.

When I first learned I was going to be a mom, my emotions ranged from pure joy to overwhelming doubt. How would I meet the expectations of my role at work while preparing to nurture a tiny human? Could I give my best to both without losing myself in the process? These questions stayed with me, lingering in my mind as I balanced pregnancy, work, and stepped into unfamiliar territory. They became the foundation of this book a space where I've poured my reflections in the hope that they resonate with others on a similar path.

This book is my way of saying, "You're not alone." I've walked this path, stumbled, and found my way time and time again. My hope is that these pages can be a source of light in your moments of doubt, a reminder that it's okay not to have it all figured out. Sleepless nights are inevitable, but they often lead to brighter days both at home and at work. What matters most is approaching each challenge with the right mindset and a little compassion for yourself.

Let's be clear: this isn't about chasing the impossible dream of "having it all." It's about redefining what "all" means to you. It's about learning to find your own rhythm, letting go of the need for perfection, and celebrating the small wins that make up the big picture.

This book isn't just for mothers. It's also for fathers-to-be those who want to understand what a woman goes through during this journey. It's a reminder that a husband's support, love, and involvement can make this experience not only bearable but beautiful and meaningful for a working woman. To every mother and father out there juggling the demands of parenting and professional life, this book is for you. It's an honest glimpse into my journey, with all its highs and lows, shared in the hope that it might offer you a little light, some clarity, and perhaps even a laugh or two on the toughest days. Let's embrace the chaos, the beauty, and everything in between together.

About the Author

Aditi Agrawal is a Software Engineer with 6 years of experience in software development. She has worked in various facets of the tech industry, excelling in problem-solving, coding, and project management. However, her journey took a transformative turn with the arrival of motherhood. Going through the dual demands of a career in technology while embracing the unpredictable beauty of motherhood, Aditi has gained unique insights into how women can bloom in both their professional and personal lives.

Through her own experiences, Aditi has learned to redefine what it means to "have it all" not by achieving perfection, but by embracing imperfection, setting realistic expectations, and finding support in both her career and family. She is passionate about helping others understand that, with the right mindset and support, women can succeed in their careers without compromising the joys of motherhood.

Outside of her professional life, Aditi values time with her family, enjoys yoga as a way to recharge, and is a strong advocate for supporting working mothers in every industry.

Contents

1.
Mindset

Finding out I was going to have a baby was a surprise that disrupted my entire world. Suddenly, my bucket list, career plans, and dreams of future adventures seemed to be put on hold. It felt like diving into a sea of unknowns, where stories from friends and society painted motherhood as a journey of endless sacrifices, changing who you are and the life you live.

This REALISATION hit hard.

Things I used to enjoy or didn't notice before started to bother me. My favorite foods, the sound of my morning alarm, even the smell of rain things that were once comforting now felt strange and unsettling. It was like I was becoming someone I didn't recognize, full of doubts about whether I could even do this. Work became another battleground. Keeping up appearances while dealing with mood swings and morning sickness felt like a lonely fight. It's strange; nobody talks about how isolating it can feel, to try to stay professional while your world is spinning.

I started asking myself why. Why do we, as women, put ourselves through this? We aim high in our careers, seek love, run households, and plan families. But at what cost? It's like we're chasing an impossible standard of being a superwoman.

But is this for society or for ourselves? We always have the choice. We could choose a quieter life, focusing just on home and family. Yet, something inside us wants more. Maybe it's because we saw our moms give their all without getting the thanks they deserved. It made us want to find our worth not just at home but out in the world too.

As I stand on the brink of becoming a mother, I'm filled with a cyclone of emotions. It's a journey into the unknown, bringing with it a blend of excitement, worry, and a thousand questions about the future. This moment feels like a pivotal turning point in my life, where everything I knew and planned for is about to change in ways I can only begin to imagine. My mind is flooded with questions. There is a constant argument playing out in my head.

How will this change me? Will I recognize myself once I'm a mother?

Well, It's completely normal to reflect on such deep questions, isn't it? Think about how a seed grows into a mighty tree. Despite its transformation from a tiny seed to a towering tree, its essence – its roots, its resilience, its purpose – remains unchanged. Similarly, as we step into the realm of motherhood, our fundamental qualities – our kindness, our empathy, our ability to love – will remain constant. We might look into the mirror and see a different reflection staring back at us, but within, we'll find the same caring heart and the same determination to nurture and protect. Like the seed that grows into a tree, we'll grow into something magnificent, filled with new experiences, insights, and strengths, while still holding onto the essence of who we've always been.

But what about our dreams? Can we pursue them while ensuring our children have everything they need? Dreams are so important, aren't they? They're like the stars guiding us through life's journey. They inspire us to reach for the sky. But you know, chasing our dreams doesn't mean we have to hit pause on life. Think about when we left home for college. Remember how scary it felt? Leaving behind everything familiar to chase our dreams? It was tough, but we did it. And it was worth it, right?

Now, think about another big leap leaving our home to start a life with our husband. It was a cyclone of emotions, wasn't it? The comfort of our childhood home, the safety of our parents' care it was hard to let go. But we took that step, trusting in love, building a new life, and creating a home together. It wasn't without its challenges, but it shaped us, made us stronger, and gave us a partner to share this journey with.

Now, as we're getting ready to become a mom, it's yet another new adventure. It's exciting, but it's also a bit daunting. We're wondering if we'll still have time for our dreams. Well, guess what? We will. Just like we embraced the unknown before, whether it was leaving for college or starting a new life with our husband, we'll navigate this new chapter too.

Motherhood doesn't mean leaving our dreams behind. It means finding new ways to pursue them, and adapting to the rhythm of a life that now includes a little one. We've done it before, and we'll do it again. It might not always be easy, but it will be worth it because life is about embracing every adventure, and every change, and finding joy and purpose in the journey.

Sure, it'll take some juggling. We'll have to get creative with our time and maybe make some adjustments. But just like we've tackled challenges before, we'll figure this out too. It might take a little while to find our groove, but we'll get there. So let's not worry too much. We've got this. We'll embrace motherhood with all its joys and challenges, and we'll keep chasing our dreams along the way. After all, that's what life's all about, isn't it?

How will my relationship evolve? Will we grow together or start drifting apart under the weight of new responsibilities? It's normal to wonder about our relationship with the big changes coming our way. But let's think about it positively. We've been through so much together, haven't we? From the highs to the lows, we've stuck together. We stood by each other's side through it all.

Now, with parenthood on the horizon, it's a whole new adventure. Sure, there will be challenges, but think about all the joy it'll bring! Those late-night giggles and shared moments will make it all worth it.

Some nights are unbearable, with sleep slipping away as my thoughts take over completely. My mind was racing with all these questions, keeping me awake for hours. It's like my worries had a life of their own, and they just wouldn't leave me alone.

Why is my mind always on overdrive? I know the answers deep down, don't I? But somehow, accepting them feels like this endless battle with myself. It's like my thoughts are at war, and I just want some peace in the chaos. I kept telling myself, "Everything will be okay". We've figured things out before, haven't we? But then there's that tiny, stubborn voice in the back of my head, refusing to listen. Why am I stuck in this loop of worry?

Maybe it's because these worries feel alive like they're feeding off my fears and doubts. But wait... isn't it okay to feel scared? To have doubts? Especially about something as monumental as becoming a parent. Yeah, maybe that's it. Maybe I just need to permit myself to feel everything the fear, the uncertainty, all of it. Maybe then, I'll finally find some rest and quiet those endless thoughts. That's it, isn't it? The first step is admitting I'm scared. Letting myself feel it. Maybe once I do, I can start letting go of the weight of these worries and shift my focus to finding real solutions.

The weight of constant worry and the endless stream of "what-ifs" had taken a heavy toll on me. I found myself withdrawing from those around me, not wanting to talk to anyone. Irritation seemed to take over my days, and I felt trapped in a relentless cycle of overthinking.

During this overwhelming phase, I turned to my ever-reliable friend Google. Typing "Overthinking during pregnancy" into the search bar felt like a desperate attempt to understand what was happening to me. The first article I clicked on explained that it was normal behavior, a common experience for many pregnant women, and attributed it to hormonal changes. That sounded reassuring, even validating. But as I scrolled further, I came across a line that stopped me cold: Too much stress can harm the baby.

Those words hit me like a thunderbolt. Harm the baby? I don't know why, but something deep within me stirred at that moment. I realized how careless I had been, allowing my own emotions and insecurities to spiral out of control. There is a life growing inside me completely dependent on me for its well-being. I couldn't let this cycle continue.

That realization brought with it a wave of clarity. Feeling irritated with the people around me, pushing them away, and wallowing in my thoughts wasn't solving anything. In fact, I was not only making my own life harder but unknowingly affecting the lives of those I cared about most and my baby. That was the moment the mother within me was born.

I began to understand that motherhood isn't just about nurturing a child when they are in your arms; it starts the moment you decide to bring them into this world. It's about creating a healthy space for them, physically, emotionally, and mentally. That realization became the catalyst for change.

I started small. The first step was to consciously pause whenever I felt myself slipping into a cycle of worry. I'd take a deep breath and remind myself that this moment, right here and now, was what mattered most. I also began journaling writing down my thoughts to see them more clearly. Putting my worries on paper somehow made them feel less daunting, less all-consuming.

I spoke to my husband about how I was feeling, and his reassuring words became my anchor. He reminded me that

I didn't have to shoulder all this alone. It was okay to feel scared, but it was also okay to let those fears go. I began to lean on his support and the support of my family, understanding that my emotions didn't define me they were simply part of my journey.

Slowly but surely, I took steps to bring positivity back into my life. I revisited old hobbies reading books that inspired me, listening to soothing music, and practicing meditation. I realized how much peace these little activities could bring. I also started affirming to myself daily: I am strong. I am capable. My baby deserves the best version of me, and I can be that for them. This mindset shift wasn't just about pregnancy; it was about preparing for the kind of parent I wanted to be someone who embraces challenges with grace and faces the unknown with courage.

As I bring this chapter to a close, I want to share something that stayed with me: it's okay to feel uncertain, to have moments where everything feels overwhelming. I had my share of those moments, and they taught me something significant. My baby didn't need a perfect version of me just a present, loving, and positive one.

This realization wasn't the end of my journey; it was the start. I had to learn, unlearn, and rediscover parts of myself I didn't even know existed. And while it wasn't always easy, every step brought me closer to becoming the mother I wanted to be.

But this is just the beginning. There's so much more to unpack about finding balance between my personal life, my work, and motherhood, overcoming fear, and embracing the unexpected joys of this journey. It's not about perfection; it's about learning to navigate all the different roles we play. So, stay with me. The road ahead is filled with lessons, laughter, and maybe even a few tears. Let's explore it together.

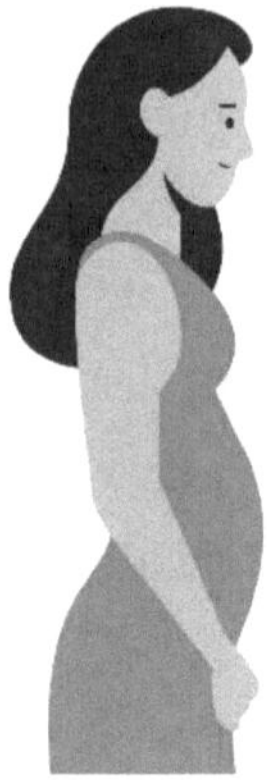

2.
First Trimester

Every woman's experience with pregnancy is different. For some, it's a bumpy road, full of challenges like morning sickness, fatigue, or unexpected health scares. For others, the path is smoother, with just the usual ups and downs that come with growing a new life. And even the same woman can have wildly different experiences with each pregnancy no two are the same. One might be a breeze, while another could come with more twists and turns than she ever imagined. Managing pregnancy while working can feel like a balancing act, and it only gets more challenging as time goes on. Each week brings new changes that can catch you off guard your body feels different, hormones are all over the place, and moods swing like a pendulum. Some days, you might find yourself smiling for no reason, feeling a rush of excitement about life growing inside you. On other days, you could be battling a short fuse or find yourself so drained that even the thought of getting out of bed seems like a task. But through it all, you have to make sure that your work doesn't take a toll on your health because as much as you might want to give your best at work, you've got to save some of that energy for yourself and your little one.

You'll probably hear a lot of advice during this time family, friends, colleagues, and even strangers seem to have endless tips and suggestions as if suddenly everyone's an expert. Some will insist you should rest more, while others might say you need to keep active. The lectures can feel overwhelming like they never seem to end. But here's the thing: the best advice is the one that comes from within. Listen to yourself. Do what you're comfortable with, what your body can handle, and most importantly, what brings you peace and happiness. Because at the end of the day, only you know what feels right for you and your baby. Trust that intuition, and let it guide you through the noise.

Finding out you're pregnant is a surreal moment. At first, it's all smiles, happy tears, and excitement with your family. But then, reality kicks in, and you start noticing all the little changes happening inside you. Those hormones start to shift, and suddenly, you don't feel quite like yourself anymore. Foods you used to crave can become downright repulsive, and you might find yourself feeling queasy, dizzy, or dealing with relentless nausea that makes you want to throw in the towel some days. Along with that, you might be dragging through the day, feeling like you could sleep for hours no matter how much rest you get. And with all this, the added pressure of keeping up at work just makes it more overwhelming.

I've always been a huge tea enthusiast my mornings practically began with the aroma of freshly brewed chai. But during my first trimester, everything changed. Even the smell of tea wafting through the kitchen was enough to send me running for the bathroom. It felt like I was suddenly allergic to my favorite thing. And since caffeine isn't exactly encouraged during pregnancy, I guess it was a blessing in disguise. Otherwise, I would have been longing for a cup every single day, missing that familiar comfort. Now, without my regular caffeine fix no tea, no coffee I found myself dragging through those long afternoons, especially at work. Being a software engineer means staring at screens and debugging code all day, and I really missed those little pick-me-ups. I used to rely on a shot of black coffee to keep my brain sharp and alert. Honestly, forget the motivational speeches or cheesy quotes on productivity what I needed was caffeine and a quick power nap! But, as it turns out, caffeine can cause blood vessels in the uterus and placenta to narrow, which might reduce the blood supply to the baby and potentially slow down growth. That's why you'll hear it from all sides your parents, in-laws, even the doctors everyone will remind you to lay off the coffee.

If you're like me and love your daily brew, it's tough to give it up all at once. So, take it easy on yourself. Start by cutting back to one or two cups a day, and slowly wean off. Trust me, quitting it abruptly just makes you crave it more, and that can be a struggle. And it's not just about tea your taste buds can pull a complete 360 degree during those early months. Foods that used to be your go-to can suddenly taste weird, or even the thought of them can make you queasy. But hey, that's all just part of the wild ride that is the first trimester. Stick with me, because in the chapters to come, you'll dive deeper into how to juggle work, health, and relationships. Everything takes a turn, and the real journey begins as we work through the challenges, embrace the changes, and realize how to balance it all. Trust me, the journey is as beautiful as the destination.

3. Workplace Battle

Finding out that you're pregnant is one of the most life-altering moments a woman can experience. Amid the excitement and joy, there's often an undercurrent of uncertainty, especially when it comes to balancing your career and this new chapter of your life. The workplace, where we spend so much of our time, plays a huge role in how smoothly this transition happens. When work is understanding and flexible, it makes all the difference in how we manage both our personal lives and careers. On the other hand, a lack of support can just add unnecessary stress, making an already challenging time even harder to navigate. It really shows how crucial a supportive and empathetic work environment is during life's big transitions.

When you first discover you're pregnant, you begin to view your job and work environment through a completely different lens. It's no longer just about deadlines, promotions, and other career goals, it becomes about your well-being and the new life growing inside of you. This is where the importance of being in a company that prioritizes a robust maternity leave policy and fosters a stress-free, supportive environment comes into sharp focus. Sharing your pregnancy news, no matter how exciting, can be a nerve-wracking experience, and having a workplace that values both the employee and the person behind the role is crucial for your mental peace during this delicate time.

A supportive work culture goes beyond just policies; it extends to the people you work with daily. During pregnancy, having a compassionate and understanding manager is invaluable. A manager who not only hears but truly understands the physical and emotional changes you're experiencing can ease much of the stress associated with juggling professional responsibilities while preparing for motherhood. Having a team that understands what you're going through and offers both emotional and practical support can really make a huge difference. Instead of facing a stressful time on your own, it feels comforting to know that people have your back. Whether it's a kind word, a helping hand, or just being there to listen, their support turns what could be a tough situation into something more manageable. It gives you a sense of being cared for, and more importantly, it empowers you to get through it, knowing you're not alone in this journey.

When I found out I was pregnant, my mind immediately began racing with thoughts, many of them filled with fear and anxiety. This pregnancy wasn't planned, and it had only been two months since I'd received a hard-earned promotion at work. At first, I couldn't feel the joy that comes with such news. Instead, I was consumed by a deluge of concerns: How would this affect my career trajectory? Would my manager support me, or would they see me as someone who couldn't handle additional responsibilities? What if I wasn't assigned to high-stress projects, knowing that I'd be leaving for six months of maternity leave? The anxiety I felt was overwhelming, and it seemed like every question led to more uncertainties.

I found myself questioning whether my career growth would be paused or even derailed. Would my absence create resentment among my colleagues, or would I be sidelined in important projects when I returned? The emotional chaos of facing the unknown felt exhausting. On top of it all, I feared judgment not only for the unplanned nature of my pregnancy but also for needing to step back at a time when I had just stepped up in my role.

Working in the Engineering department, I was used to being one of the few women on the team. It wasn't something I usually gave much thought to, but when I found out I was pregnant, the lack of female colleagues became more evident. Suddenly, I found myself grappling with the reality that in a field so dominated by men, there weren't many role models or support systems for someone in my situation. I had no idea who I could turn to for advice or guidance. How do you bring up something as deeply personal as pregnancy in an environment where the focus is usually on work talk, technical discussions, and looming project deadlines?

The male dominance in the field added another layer of complexity. In an environment where the culture often revolves around long hours, constant problem-solving, and a "work through everything" mentality, it felt like I was stepping into uncharted territory. There was no one I could relate to directly, no one who understood the balance between pregnancy and work that I was now facing. At times, I felt isolated, like I was carrying this massive secret. It felt like I was the only one in the room who was juggling this new reality of pregnancy with the usual pressures of work. I didn't know how to ask for flexibility or understanding without feeling like I was asking for too much.

The lack of open conversation about women's health, pregnancy, and work-life balance in such a male-dominated field only made it harder to find a space where

I felt comfortable. I wasn't sure how or when to share my news without feeling like I was burdening anyone.

At first, I didn't know who to talk to. Should I go directly to my manager? Should I wait until I was further along in my pregnancy? I didn't want to keep this news to myself for too long, but at the same time, I was anxious about how it would be received. I had so many thoughts racing through my mind, but no clear answers. After some internal debate, I decided to reach out to my Human Resource Business Partner (HRBP). She was the person we all went to whenever we had any work-related questions whether it was about policies, benefits, or just general team concerns.

So, I took the first step and scheduled a 1:1 meeting with her by blocking some time on her calendar. As I clicked "send" on the invite, I felt a wave of nerves wash over me. This wasn't just any conversation, it was *the* conversation that would set the tone for how my pregnancy would be managed at work. It felt huge.

The day of the meeting arrived, and as the time for our call grew closer, my heart was pounding. I had no idea how she would react or what her guidance would be. Would she see this as a complication? Or would she be supportive and understanding? I rehearsed what I was going to say in my head multiple times, wanting to strike the right balance between professionalism and personal disclosure.

When we finally got on the call, I took a deep breath and dove in. "I have some exciting news," I began, trying to keep my voice steady. "I'm going to be starting a family soon, and I wanted to discuss the next steps for how to handle this at work."

There was a brief pause on the other end of the line, and for a second, my stomach dropped. But then, she responded with a warm, "Oh, congratulations! That's wonderful news!" The weight I had been carrying immediately felt a little lighter. Her genuine happiness for me felt like a small but significant victory. I wasn't just another employee dealing with a "situation". I was a person experiencing something life-changing, and she acknowledged that with kindness.

She then walked me through the company's process for maternity leave. "I'm going to send you a document with all the details you need," she said. "It'll cover how much leave you're entitled to, when you need to notify your manager, and how to handle the transition," she added. Her tone was calm and supportive, which was exactly what I needed at that moment.

Later that day, I received the document in my inbox and sat down to read through it. It outlined everything clearly the number of days I was entitled to, how to apply for leave, and the timelines for notifying my manager. But as useful as the document was, it wasn't the most important part of that day. What truly stood out to me was the way she made me feel during our conversation. She didn't just pass along policy information; she took the time to listen, reassure me, and to make sure I felt comfortable.

Before we ended our call, she gave me some advice that stuck with me. "When you feel ready," she said, "you can start planning how to communicate this with your manager. Take your time, and whenever you're comfortable, we'll support you." Her words felt like a gentle reminder that I wasn't alone in this process. She wasn't rushing me or pressuring me to take immediate action, but instead, she gave me space to process things on my own terms.

That simple exchange left a lasting impact. It was such a relief to know that there was someone at work who truly had my back, and who was there to help me figure out how to handle pregnancy while managing my work life. In a department where I didn't have many female colleagues to relate to, having this kind of support made all the difference. It was at that moment that I realized how crucial it is to have not just policies, but people, who care.

Now that I had a better understanding of the company policies, the next big question looming in my mind was, *How do I talk to my manager about this?* Having recently been promoted, I was still adjusting to working with a new manager. I didn't have the same rapport with him as I did with my previous managers, and that made me hesitant. I kept overthinking the situation, replaying different scenarios in my head. How would he take the news? Would this affect how he viewed me professionally? I started making the conversation into a much bigger deal than it probably was, but I couldn't help it. The uncertainty was eating at me.

In my state of confusion, I thought of my previous manager, the one I had worked with for years, the one I was still comfortable talking to. I felt like he'd have the perfect advice for me since he knew me so well. Without overthinking it, I decided to message him. He was always approachable, and I figured he'd be the right person to guide me through this.

As expected, he was just one ping away. Within minutes of reaching out, he responded, and before I knew it, we were on a call. It felt so easy and natural to talk to him, which immediately put me at ease. After catching up a little, I shared my big news. He was genuinely happy for me and congratulated me warmly. That small exchange reminded me why I had always appreciated him as a manager, he cared, not just about the work, but about the people behind it.

I then told him about my concerns, how I wasn't sure how to approach my new manager or when to bring up the conversation. I asked him, "How do I even start this discussion? And when's the best time to do it?"

His response was exactly what I needed to hear. "It's no big deal," he said, his tone calm and reassuring. "Don't overthink it. Just go ahead and tell your new manager, and you can both plan it out from there. It's really as simple as that."

Hearing those words from someone I trusted made all the difference. He made it sound so straightforward, and I realized I had been building up the whole thing too much.

Once my first trimester was over, I finally felt like it was the right time to have that important conversation with my manager during our 1:1 meeting. In my organization, we had these bi-weekly check-ins where we'd go over company priorities, ongoing projects, and any other issues that needed attention. It was one of those rare chances to bring up anything personal too, whether it was a challenge I was facing or a request for support. And now, I have something really big to share.

The day finally came when I had to share the news. I was nervous but knew it had to be done. We started our 1:1 as usual, diving into the projects I was handling, what was coming up next, and my deliverables. It was all the usual work talk at first. Then, we shifted gears a bit, moving into the more casual side of the conversation chit-chat about life, and then the question came: "So, anything new going on in your life?"

That question hit me like a wave. My mind went blank, and for a split second, I just sat there, frozen. But I knew this was my chance, and I couldn't keep it in any longer. I took a deep breath, steadied myself, and managed to say,

"Yeah, actually, I have some really big news. I'm going to be starting a family soon." I tried to keep my tone upbeat, but I couldn't help the nervousness that crept into my voice. "I'm excited, but honestly, I'm a little nervous too wondering how all of this will affect my work, how I'll manage everything with this big change on the horizon."

He listened quietly as I spoke, giving me the space to get it all out. When I finished, he didn't jump straight into work-related concerns or logistics, which I'd been so worried about. Instead, he paused, and then with a warm smile, said, "Hey, congratulations! That's amazing news, I'm so happy for you." His words felt like a weight lifting off my shoulders, and I couldn't help but smile back, feeling a little more at ease.

He went on, "I understand what you're going through. You know, it reminds me of when I was expecting my first child. Even as a dad, it was such a nerve-wracking time. I was full of uncertainty. I can only imagine how much more it must feel like that for you." He paused as if choosing his words carefully.

"But look, don't worry too much about work right now. Your health, your well-being, that comes first. If you need time off or if there are days when you just can't make it, just send me a quick message, even if you can't get it through the Workday system."

He leaned back as if trying to take the weight off my shoulders with his own words. "This is a life-changing experience for you, and you deserve to enjoy it fully. Work will always be here, and I won't sugarcoat it, there'll be challenges, but if it ever becomes too much or if it's affecting you, let's work together to find a solution. We'll make it work."

As he spoke, I felt this warmth spreading inside me, like a burden I hadn't even realized I was carrying had been lightened. His empathy and understanding made all the difference, and I found myself sitting there, taking in his words, feeling genuinely seen and supported. I'll always be grateful for that conversation and for the way, he supported me throughout my pregnancy. It's something I'll carry with me, knowing that not everyone has the same experience. I sincerely wish that every woman in a similar situation could have a manager who's as understanding and supportive.

Having a manager who genuinely cares can make a world of difference. It's like having a safety net reassurance that someone has your back even on the toughest days. That kind of support doesn't just motivate you to give your best; it fosters a sense of gratitude and belonging. You feel seen and valued not just as an employee but as a person navigating one of life's most profound transitions. At the same time, I came to understand that this support isn't something to take for granted. It requires honesty about your health and limitations, even when it's uncomfortable to admit you're struggling. Pretending everything is fine when it's not can strain the trust and understanding that's been built. By being transparent about your needs and respecting the kindness shown to you, you create a relationship of mutual respect a foundation for navigating challenges together.

But not everyone has the privilege of understanding leadership. In some workplaces, the absence of support can make pregnancy feel isolating and overwhelming. If you find yourself in this situation, it's important to take proactive steps to advocate for yourself. Start by reaching out to your HR team to understand the policies, benefits, and protections available. If conversations with your manager aren't productive, document those interactions. Keeping a clear record can be a powerful tool for ensuring your concerns are acknowledged.

What happens, though, when the situation crosses into unfair treatment or discrimination? This is where knowing your rights becomes crucial. Many countries have workplace laws that safeguard pregnant employees against mistreatment. Don't hesitate to seek advice from legal experts or organizations specializing in employee rights. Simultaneously, lean on your personal support system whether it's family, friends, or online communities of working parents to help you navigate these challenges.

If your workplace constantly feels unsupportive or toxic, the thought of switching jobs might cross your mind. It's not an easy decision, especially during pregnancy, but it can be a necessary one for your mental and physical well-being. Before making a move, carefully evaluate potential employers. Look for organizations with policies and cultures that support working parents. Ask about flexibility, parental leave, and how they accommodate transitions like yours.

That said, switching jobs during pregnancy isn't always the best or easiest option. It's a balance of assessing your current situation, exploring alternatives, and planning for a future that aligns with your needs and values. Ultimately, whether you decide to stay and advocate for change or make the leap to a new opportunity, the priority should always be your health, well-being, and the safe arrival of your baby. You deserve an environment where you're supported, valued, and empowered to thrive both personally and professionally.

4.
The Dad to be....

To all the amazing pregnant women out there, remember that it's not just us who are going through this journey. Our partners the soon-to-be fathers are right there with us. From the moment we find out we're expecting, they share in the excitement and the challenges of bringing a new life into the world. From the very beginning, our partners stand by our side, helping us handle the emotional ups and downs that pregnancy often brings. It's not easy dealing with mood swings and the many changes in our bodies, but our partners are often our support system. They're there to keep us calm when we feel anxious, to hold us close when we're overwhelmed, and to reassure us when worries take over.

It's important to remember that they have their own internal struggles, too. Just like us, they might feel a mix of emotions excitement, fear, anticipation, and love but they might not always have the chance to talk about them. Society often expects men to be strong and silent during pregnancy, which can leave them feeling alone in their experience. They might worry about fatherhood and how they'll provide for their growing family.

Men can also go through physical changes during pregnancy, though they show up differently than ours. They might have symptoms like constipation, gas, and bloating, which can be physical signs of stress and anxiety about the changes ahead. These are normal responses to the new responsibilities and pressures that come with becoming a dad. While we deal with the physical changes of pregnancy, our partners often experience these changes more mentally and emotionally. They might not endure the physical symptoms we do, but their journey is just as significant. They may not carry the child physically, but they carry the emotional weight and responsibilities with equal importance.

I remember how deeply connected my husband and I became during my pregnancy. It was as if we were both experiencing everything together, side by side. On nights when he struggled to sleep, I found myself lying awake too, caught in his restlessness. The same happened when I struggled with any pain or evening sickness, he lay wide awake helping me fall asleep. This sense of shared unease became even more evident when the baby was especially active, moving as though part of our midnight watchfulness. In those quiet, sleepless hours, I realized just how deeply interconnected we were, each in harmony with the other's emotions and steering through this journey together in silent unity. Those restless nights were not just about the baby kicking; they were moments when we lay awake, talking quietly about our hopes and fears for the future. Sometimes, the simple act of feeling the baby's movements together made us pause and realize how real everything was becoming. When my husband seemed worried or distracted, it affected my mood as well. His anxiety about becoming a father and his desire to support me in every way possible were things he often kept to himself. However, I could sense the weight he carried, and it was hard for me to see him struggle in silence. We learned to communicate more openly about our feelings, which strengthened our bond even further. This mutual support was crucial for us, helping us both deal with the uncertainties of pregnancy.

5.
Partner's Worklife

Pregnancy doesn't just bring changes for the expectant mother it significantly impacts the partner's life as well, particularly when it comes to work routines and priorities. My husband, for instance, had a demanding job that required late-night check-ins, deployments, and handling production issues a routine that's all too common for those in the engineering field. These erratic hours had become a way of life for him. However, once we discovered the pregnancy, we realized the need to make changes for the sake of our health and well-being.

One of the first adjustments we focused on was establishing a healthier bedtime routine. Initially, we set a target to be in bed by 1 a.m., gradually working towards wrapping up all tasks by 11 p.m. It wasn't easy and certainly didn't happen overnight it took about two weeks of consistent effort to adjust. Keeping phones and laptops aside was an essential part of this change, as these gadgets emit radio waves that could potentially affect the baby's development and our own mental health. This simple yet crucial step not only improved our sleep quality but also created a more mindful environment for us as a couple preparing for parenthood.

Beyond the schedule changes, my husband's career priorities underwent a significant transformation. He had been contemplating a job switch for some time, looking for growth and new challenges. However, after hearing the news of the baby, his perspective shifted. He chose to prioritize the stability and work-life balance of his current role over the uncertainty of a new job. He had built a good reputation and camaraderie with his teammates, and he decided that being comfortable in his role was more important during this critical time. This shift in mindset wasn't just practical; it spoke volumes about the emotional and psychological adjustments he made as he prepared for the lifelong responsibility of parenthood.

While managing his work responsibilities, my husband was always attuned to my needs during pregnancy. One thing he quickly noticed was how my tailbone pain, which worsened during the second trimester, was making it nearly impossible for me to sit for long hours at my desk.

It wasn't something I openly complained about, but he could see the toll it was taking on me, both physically and mentally. Balancing my work while enduring that discomfort was becoming increasingly challenging, and it was starting to affect my focus and productivity. Without hesitation, he came up with a thoughtful solution – setting up a "work-from-bed" arrangement that completely transformed my daily routine. He didn't just stop at placing a table by the bed; he took extra care to make sure it was perfect. He carefully selected the most comfortable pillows to support my back and neck, ensuring I could maintain the right posture while working. He even adjusted the height of the table so my legs wouldn't dangle off the edge of the bed, a small detail that made a huge difference in easing my discomfort.

But he didn't stop there. Understanding that I needed to stay connected and functional, he arranged for power cords for my laptop, ensuring I could work uninterrupted. At the same time, he made sure the setup allowed me to easily get up whenever I needed to, without feeling bed-bound. It was more than just a solution; it was a thoughtful effort to make sure I stayed comfortable, and productive, and never felt restricted by my circumstances.

His attention to detail and care made a world of difference. I finally felt supported, both literally and emotionally, as I could now work without the constant distraction of pain. It wasn't just about solving a physical issue – it was his way of showing how deeply he cared about my well-being. That simple yet impactful change allowed me to feel more at ease, which in turn boosted my productivity and helped me find a balance that I had been struggling to achieve.

These adjustments in our routines and the care we put into supporting each other really showed me how much the arrival of a baby affects both parents not just the mother. It also raised a question that I often ponder: is it fair for fathers to have only two weeks of paternity leave, compared to the six months (or more) that mothers typically receive for maternity leave? Two weeks is a woefully short time. It barely allows fathers to process the overwhelming changes, let alone adequately support their recovering partner and bond with the newborn. As a working woman, I was entitled to six months of maternity leave a time frame designed to allow mothers to recover from childbirth, bond with the newborn, and adjust to the new role of parenting. On the other hand, my husband was given just two weeks of paternity leave.

Two weeks. Fourteen days. It's a short span when you consider what those early days entail. Recovery from childbirth often takes weeks, sometimes months, depending on the delivery method and any complications. Meanwhile, the newborn requires constant attention feeding, diaper changes, and the soothing presence of parents. Two weeks barely scratches the surface of the support a mother and child need from their partner. During this period, my husband was not just my emotional anchor; he was also the one managing household responsibilities, running errands, and ensuring I had everything I needed to recover. He was my bridge to the outside world while I healed, and he was the first to experience some of the chaos and joys of our baby's arrival. Yet, just as we started to find our rhythm, his leave ended, and he had to return to work.

This limitation forced us to think about how to manage the postpartum phase. We coordinated with both my family and my husband's, dividing responsibilities as best as we could. But it also left us wondering: why is paternity leave so short? Why do policies fail to recognize that fathers, too, need time to bond with their children and support their partners during this crucial phase? A longer paternity leave would not just benefit fathers but the entire family. It would provide the partner with more time to adjust to the life-changing responsibilities of parenthood. It would create opportunities for stronger family bonds to form early on. For the mother, it would offer much-needed relief from the overwhelming demands of recovery and newborn care.

6.
Partner's contributions

Your partner plays an essential role in this pregnancy journey. It's not just about how much your husband earns or what he can provide financially; it's about the support, love, and care he offers every day. The emotional support a partner provides can be just as important, if not more so, than financial stability. Little gestures can make a big difference during this time, and they show how invested he is in the journey. For instance, it's extremely comforting to have someone who makes sure you're taking your vitamins and medications on time. Those gentle reminders are not just about health; they're a way of showing that he cares about you and the baby. It's the simple act of someone looking out for you, understanding that your well-being is intertwined with theirs.

Pregnancy can be overwhelming, with so many appointments, check-ups, and things to keep track of. My husband played a crucial role in helping me stay organized, especially when it came to managing doctor visits and ultrasounds. He would add every appointment to our shared Google Calendar, setting up reminders to ensure we didn't miss anything. He was careful to schedule them in a way that wouldn't disrupt either of our work commitments, which made everything feel less chaotic. Beyond this, he also took charge of what I ate, making sure I had nutritious meals and healthy snacks readily available. These thoughtful actions reflected his deep commitment to not only supporting me but also sharing the responsibility of this life-changing experience.

Every night before we went to bed, my husband made it a point to ensure we were both eating right and healthy. It became part of our nightly routine a quiet moment where he would double-check that our diet was aligned with the recommendations from my doctor. I remember feeling overwhelmed by the constant stream of dietary advice and the pressure to follow every guideline perfectly. My husband took it upon himself to help me navigate through these nutritional demands. He became the mastermind behind our meals, ensuring that I was getting all the essential nutrients. Each day, he'd avail a variety of foods coconut water, spinach, fresh fruits, green vegetables, and dry fruits. These were not just items on a list; they were carefully chosen to support my health and our baby's development.

One of the biggest challenges was avoiding foods that weren't suitable for pregnancy, especially since I have a love for Chinese cuisine. I have always enjoyed the rich flavors and variety of Chinese dishes, but many of them use MSG (Ajinomoto), which isn't recommended during pregnancy. My husband was incredibly attentive to this concern. He made sure that we didn't have any Chinese food that contained MSG, replacing it with homemade versions that were both delicious and safe. There were times when sticking to this regimen felt challenging, especially when I was craving the comforting flavors of Chinese food. My husband would gently remind me why avoiding MSG was important, not just for my health but for our babies as well, ensuring that our meals were both satisfying and nutritious.

What truly stood out was his willingness to sacrifice his own culinary preferences to make sure I stayed motivated. On some days, he would forgo his favorite dishes and join me in eating simple khichdi a humble yet nutritious meal that adhered to our dietary guidelines. Watching him set aside his taste buds and enjoy the same simple food as I did was incredibly motivating. His efforts didn't go unnoticed. It wasn't just about the food; it was about the love and dedication he put into ensuring that we both were following a healthy lifestyle. Every meal we shared, and every dietary choice we made together, reinforced the bond between us. His support and willingness to make these adjustments for me made me feel cared for and understood, turning what could have been a stressful experience into a shared journey of wellness. By committing to this routine together, including avoiding my favorite Chinese dishes with MSG, we created a supportive environment that made the dietary demands of pregnancy more manageable. His involvement transformed the experience from one of individual responsibility to a joint effort, making the journey to parenthood even more meaningful.

Sharing responsibilities equally is perhaps one of the most important aspects of being a supportive partner. This includes everything from household chores to attending prenatal classes together. When a partner steps up and shares the load, it lightens the physical and emotional burden that often comes with pregnancy. It's about being a team and working together to create a loving and nurturing environment for your growing family. I've noticed that the most meaningful support often comes from these small acts of kindness and consideration. They remind you that you're not alone in this journey and that your partner is genuinely invested in the well-being of both you and the baby.

Ultimately, a supportive partner is someone who listens, understands, and stands by your side through every high and low. It's about building a foundation of love and trust that will carry you both into parenthood. Knowing you have someone who is as excited and committed as you are makes the experience of pregnancy all the more rewarding.

I noticed that this journey brought out a more caring and empathetic side in both of us. We became more attuned to each other's needs, understanding that pregnancy was not just my experience but ours. It taught us the importance of leaning on one another and trusting that we were both doing our best to prepare for the arrival of our child. This shared journey was a powerful reminder of what it means to be truly connected with someone, to share in their joys and burdens, and to grow together as a couple. It made me appreciate the incredible bond we had, knowing that we were creating not just a child, but also a family.

7.
Second Trimester

The second trimester, often referred to as the "babymoon phase" of pregnancy, brought a wave of renewal for both me and my husband. After a challenging first trimester, when morning sickness and a rollercoaster of mood swings made each day feel long, this new phase was a welcome change. Gone were the days when my favorite foods seemed like adversaries I began to enjoy my meals again, savoring flavors and experiencing the return of my usual energy. Physically, I started showing, and I could feel the faintest movements of my little one, like gentle flutters that made everything feel so real. It was a period of calm and joy, not just for me but also for my husband, who cherished these precious moments with me.

By now, the nausea and constant fatigue that had plagued me seemed to fade into the background. My body started adjusting to the changes, and I could finally indulge in the simple pleasures of food again. The cravings shifted, and I could actually taste and enjoy meals without the dread of an upset stomach afterward. What was even more comforting was how my energy levels seemed to skyrocket, a complete contrast to the previous months. It felt like I had my life back, at least for a little while.

Physically, the changes in my body became more visible. My belly began to round out, and I started to show in a way that made the pregnancy feel so much more real. With every gentle flutter of my baby's movements, I felt an overwhelming sense of connection to the life inside me. Those first little kicks, those tender nudges, were like a sweet secret between my baby and me. It was as if the world slowed down in those moments, and I could fully embrace the miracle of what was happening. There were no more doubts, no more fears just pure, unadulterated joy.

This period also marked a shift in my professional life. I felt surprisingly productive and focused, something that, a few months ago, I wouldn't have imagined possible. I was back at work, feeling more in control and more capable than I had in the first trimester. My brain, which had been in a fog of fatigue and discomfort, felt clear again. I was completing my tasks on time, attending meetings with energy, and keeping up with deadlines at a pace I hadn't experienced in months. There was something deeply satisfying about this. Pregnancy, which I thought might slow me down, had actually given me an unexpected boost. The sense of accomplishment at work, knowing I was not only handling my responsibilities but doing so with confidence, was so fulfilling. It reassured me that I could balance this monumental life change and still perform at my best.

During this phase, one major issue I faced was intense tailbone pain, which made it difficult to sit for long hours. Even simple movements like getting up and sitting down became increasingly painful, and it started to affect my daily routine. There were moments when I felt helpless, wondering if this discomfort would persist for the rest of my pregnancy. I initially turned to online research and found that tailbone pain is a common symptom during pregnancy, but it still left me worried. My husband and I decided it was best to consult our doctor for advice.

When we discussed it with her, she reassured us that this was a normal symptom during pregnancy. She explained that as the baby grows, the increasing weight and pressure shift the body's center of gravity, changing posture and putting extra strain on the tailbone. On top of that, pregnancy hormones like relaxin play a role. Relaxin is released to loosen the ligaments and joints in the pelvic area, preparing the body for childbirth. While this flexibility is necessary, it can also cause instability and lead to pain in areas like the tailbone. In my case, the combination of these factors was contributing to my discomfort. However, she also informed us that painkillers weren't an option, as they could have adverse effects on the baby's development. Instead, she suggested practical alternatives: using a tailbone pillow to ease the pressure and ensuring my legs were parallel to the floor rather than hanging down, which could intensify the pain.

We took her advice seriously. My husband, as always, stepped in to make things easier for me. As I shared in my last chapter, the comfortable work-from-bed arrangement he thoughtfully set up with a tailbone pillow, a table, and a chair adjusted to keep my legs in the right position proved to be an invaluable asset during this phase. It alleviated much of the discomfort and allowed me to continue working more comfortably and efficiently for the rest of my pregnancy. These adjustments, combined with his care and unwavering support, became a cornerstone of my ability to stay productive and feel supported during this challenging time.

My job had always encouraged me to ask the 'why' behind everything, and this habit carried over into my pregnancy. I found myself curious about every change happening in my body why I was feeling certain pains, why I needed to rest more, and what was causing these symptoms. Educating myself about the science behind these changes gave me a sense of control and reassurance.

Understanding the logic behind my tailbone pain made it easier to accept and deal with it. Instead of feeling helpless, I could approach the discomfort with a more practical and informed mindset, which made a big difference in how I managed the journey.

It wasn't just my career that flourished in this phase. The connection between my husband and me deepened, and we relished in this time of harmony. It was our "couple time," a gift that felt even more precious as we knew life would soon change with the arrival of our baby. We enjoyed long talks, spontaneous outings, and quiet evenings, savoring the last moments of just the two of us.

It was also the phase where we made big decisions for the future like our move to a new city. His work-from-home arrangement was ending, and we knew it was time to relocate. Although the timing felt intense with my pregnancy, we knew it was a necessary step.

Moving homes, especially during pregnancy, seemed daunting at first, but we approached it with a sense of purpose and teamwork. We carefully planned every detail, ensuring that the process would be smooth without overwhelming ourselves. I took two days off from work to focus entirely on the move, and surprisingly, it went without a hitch. We had our share of stressful moments, of course, but we worked together and supported each other every step of the way. The support from my work team and manager was invaluable they understood the balancing act I was managing and encouraged me to take the time I needed without stress.

Looking back on the second trimester, I can honestly say it was my favorite part of the pregnancy. It felt like a golden period where everything fell into place. I was thriving in my career, enjoying precious moments with my family, and basking in the anticipation of the new chapter of life we were about to start. Every day was filled with a sense of balance, accomplishment, and love, and it made the challenges of the first trimester feel worth it. This phase of pregnancy not only helped me physically but also emotionally and mentally. I felt like I was finally in my element connected to myself, my family, and my work. It was the perfect time to cherish the present while preparing for the future. I don't think I've ever felt more grounded and at peace than I did during those months.

What lies ahead is a mix of preparation, reflection, and moments that will leave a lasting impact. The journey continues, and I can't wait to share it with you.

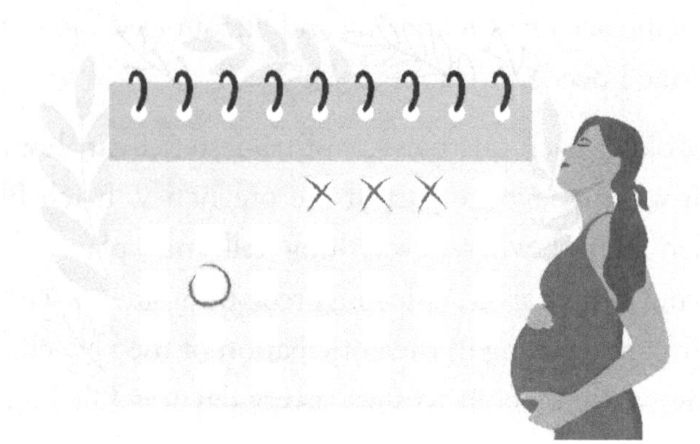

8.
Planning Maternity

Planning for maternity leave is one of the first big steps on the journey to becoming a mother, which requires careful consideration of personal and professional priorities. It's a time filled with excitement, nerves, and questions: How long should I take off? When should I start my leave? What will happen while I'm away from work? Like many working mothers, I found myself grappling with these questions as I approached the final trimester of pregnancy.

Before diving into logistics, I began by familiarizing myself with my company's maternity leave policy, something every expecting mother should do as early as possible. I live in India, where the Maternity Benefit Act 1961 is the legal framework. I knew I was entitled to 26 weeks of leave for each of my first two children and 12 weeks for any subsequent children. However, I quickly learned that while the law provides a baseline, company policies can vary. For some women, workplaces offer additional benefits, extended leave options, or flexible arrangements, and others may have policies that don't quite align with the Act. I reached out to my Human Resource Representative to clarify my company's approach and any specific requirements to ensure I was fully informed.

Typically, to be eligible for maternity leave, two key conditions must be fulfilled. First, an employee needs to have completed at least 80 days of work in the 12 months leading up to the due date. Second, the 26 weeks of leave can be split into pre- and post-delivery periods based on personal health needs. This split offers flexibility: up to 8 weeks can be taken before the delivery, and the remaining 18 weeks after. Importantly, the policy provides 26 weeks of leave for each child, not a cumulative total across multiple pregnancies. However, the exact balance often depends on personal circumstances, health conditions, and, in some cases, the organization's policies. I appreciated the flexibility this offered, even if it left me with more choices to weigh.

In the back of my mind, I felt torn between maximizing my time off with my newborn and ensuring I was rested and prepared for the birth itself. Friends, family members, and colleagues mothers who had been through this journey before shared their advice and insights. Many suggested that I consider starting my leave by the ninth month, giving me time to rest, recharge, and prepare physically and mentally for the big day. They shared how the final stretch of pregnancy is often the most challenging physically, as the baby's rapid growth can make day-to-day activities difficult. I listened to their stories of swollen feet, restless nights, and the emotional ups and downs that come with the body's changes. I listened to each perspective carefully, noting down their suggestions and experiences. Their words helped me start strategizing how to structure my leave in a way that balanced my health, my baby's needs, and the transition back to work.

Yet, as helpful as their advice was, I felt a pull in another direction. Work had become a refuge of sorts, a comforting space that allowed me to focus on something beyond my pregnancy. The familiar rhythm of projects and deadlines provided a sense of normalcy in an otherwise transformative time. Engaging in work tasks, even with the occasional backache or leg swelling, helped me feel productive, keeping me grounded when everything else felt like it was changing too fast. I realized that while others might prefer a slower pace toward the end, I found comfort in staying busy. I was aware that this approach wouldn't work for everyone, but it was right for me.

It made me realize that the goal is to figure out what works best for you. Every pregnancy is different, and every person's journey is unique. The important thing is to listen to yourself and make choices that feel right, trusting that you'll adapt along the way.

Still, the physical demands of late pregnancy weren't something I could ignore. The ninth month, as many had warned, introduced a whole new set of challenges. As my baby grew, so did my discomfort. The baby's weight pressed on my bladder, leading to frequent, almost constant, trips to the bathroom. My back ached, my feet swelled, and even getting a good night's sleep became a luxury I could only dream about. Sitting for prolonged periods, something my work required, became increasingly difficult. We tried everything we could to bring ease and comfort to my work routine. From experimenting with specialized chairs to rearranging pillows and adjusting my setup, every day was about finding new ways to make things more manageable. I even tried a work-from-bed setup, carefully propping myself up with pillows and arranging everything to stay productive. Each day felt like a small battle between my mind, which was ready to work, and my body, which was crying out for rest.

I decided to make a list of priorities that would guide me in my final days at work before the leave. The list served as both a to-do checklist and a way to feel in control amidst the cyclone of emotions. I focused on wrapping up projects, delegating responsibilities, and documenting important details that my team would need in my absence. Ensuring a smooth handover became a point of pride, as I wanted to know that I had left everything in good shape. There's a certain comfort in knowing that work can carry on smoothly in your absence, and I wanted to ensure that both for myself and for the team members stepping in while I was away.

Planning maternity is such a deeply personal experience, one that no one else can truly define for you. As I moved ahead in this journey, I learned that there is no universal right or wrong way to approach it just what works for you. For me, that meant staying connected to work until the last possible moment, despite the physical discomforts of the third trimester. It wasn't always easy, but I found comfort in the familiarity of work. There's something about being busy and engaged, even when your body is changing, that can make you feel grounded and in control when everything else feels uncertain.

But I also realized that this approach isn't for everyone. Some people may need to slow down earlier, and that's perfectly fine too. The most important thing is to listen to your own body and figure out what feels right for you, without the pressure of others' expectations or timelines. What I've learned is that the journey to motherhood doesn't have to follow a set path. It's about being in tune with your own needs whether that means taking a step back earlier to rest and prepare or pushing through until the last minute to stay connected. Each choice is valid, as long as it's what feels best for you.

Planning maternity is about balance: balancing work with personal needs, rest with productivity, and preparation with spontaneity. It's about respecting your body's limits while also acknowledging your own strength and resilience. And most importantly, it's about understanding that the choices you make during this time will shape your experience, so trust yourself, and know that whatever path you choose is the right one for you.

9.
Pause, Breathe, Work, Repeat...

At the beginning of my pregnancy, I was consumed with a single thought: How would I keep up with the expectations at work while navigating this new chapter of my life? It felt like a race I had been running for years, always pushing myself to meet deadlines, exceed goals, and prove my worth. But now, suddenly, my body had a different agenda. I remember the first time I noticed the physical toll pregnancy was taking on me fatigue set in deeper than ever before, my body seemed to move slower, and I couldn't shake the feeling that my mind was constantly in overdrive.

It was as if I had hit a wall, but this time, the wall wasn't something I could power through. The discomfort, the emotional rollercoaster, and the sheer weight of carrying a new life all made me rethink my approach to work. For someone who had always prided themselves on their ambition, this felt like a betrayal. How could I continue my usual pace? How could I maintain my productivity when everything in me was telling me to slow down?

I felt a constant internal conflict my ambition telling me to push through, and my body and heart urging me to pause. The pressure of being a "successful" professional and soon-to-be mother was overwhelming. I began to wonder: Is slowing down an act of failure, or is it something I need to embrace?

Before this moment, I had spent time reading about successful career-driven women many of whom had families and children. I was amazed at how they managed to thrive in their careers without letting motherhood hold them back. I wanted to understand the secret behind their balance. So, I started reading about their routines, their day-to-day habits, and how they made it all work. Whether it was a successful actress, entrepreneur, or businesswoman, one common thread stood out: they all prioritized fitness. The answer was yoga, meditation, and investing time in their well-being. It became clear to me that self-care wasn't a luxury it was the foundation for success.

At that moment, I realized something crucial: the idea of pausing didn't just seem like a luxury, it felt almost like a betrayal of my ambition. How could I align my desire to succeed at work with the need to slow down and care for myself? That's when I started thinking about how modern motherhood, while often glorified for its multitasking superpowers, doesn't always offer room for self-care especially when you're juggling a full-time career, pregnancy, and the weight of expectations.

We are the mothers of the modern era, well-informed about the benefits of yoga and meditation. The importance of these practices is echoed in countless articles, books, and even thousands of Instagram reels, all highlighting their significance for mental health. But despite this widespread awareness, do we manage to incorporate them into our daily routines? It's likely that 90% of us would answer "No." Many of us may start with good intentions, yet find it challenging to continue amidst our busy lifestyles, schedules, and routines.

So, is it a matter of not wanting to do it, or are we simply unable to carve out time for it? For most of us, the challenge lies in time management and prioritizing self-care. We possess all the necessary knowledge but often struggle to put it into practice.

As modern mothers, it's crucial to recognize that taking time for yoga and meditation isn't just another task on our to-do list it's an investment in our well-being. By redefining our schedules to include these practices, we not only enhance our own health but also set a powerful example for our families. It's about making a conscious choice to prioritize our mental and physical health every day, no matter how small the commitment might seem initially. Each moment spent on yoga and meditation is a step towards a more balanced and fulfilled life.

By the time I reached my second trimester, something within me began to shift. As you've already read in the earlier chapters about my struggles during the first trimester and the adjustments I made in the second, this was when I finally started to feel more like myself again. My body started to feel like it was mine again, and I began to see light at the end of the tunnel. It was during this time that I really started thinking about not just my own health, but my baby's too. I wanted us both to be as healthy as possible. Inspired and a bit more energetic.

I decided it was time to see if yoga and meditation could fit into my life. But with so many videos and tips online from YouTube to Instagram it was overwhelming. Everyone had an opinion, and they often contradicted each other. Knowing how different each pregnancy can be, I decided I wouldn't just follow any advice without checking first. So, at my next doctor's visit, I came prepared with a list of questions about doing yoga and meditation safely during pregnancy. I wanted to be sure any routine I took up was perfectly tailored not just for any pregnant woman, but for me and my baby, right here, right now.

The doctor asked how I had been feeling lately, and I replied, “I’m doing pretty good, actually. After the rough first three months, I finally feel like I’ve turned a corner. I’m happy, I feel normal again, and it’s like I’m getting back to my old self.” The doctor smiled and said, "Ah, you've reached what many refer to as the 'Baby Moon' phase of pregnancy. Congratulations! It’s typically the most beautiful and manageable phase for most women. It’s important to enjoy this time. Are there any specific concerns you have right now?"

I shared that I was feeling much better, but there was still one issue: "Being a software engineer, I have to sit at my computer for 7-8 hours a day, and lately, this has been causing quite a bit of tailbone and leg pain." The doctor nodded, understanding my concern, and advised, "That’s understandable. Sitting for long periods isn't ideal now. Be sure to take regular breaks get up, walk around, or even take a short nap before getting back to work. Have you thought about starting some gentle yoga and meditation? I’ve got some beginner-friendly videos on my YouTube channel that could help. I’ll send you the link."

I was relieved to hear this suggestion because I had been thinking about it too. “I’ve been reading a lot about how beneficial yoga and meditation are during pregnancy. I’ve watched a few YouTube videos, but there’s so much conflicting advice out there. Some say do this, others say do something else. It's overwhelming, and honestly, I'm afraid to follow random videos without knowing if they're right for me." The doctor reassured me, saying, "I completely understand. That's exactly why I started my YouTube channel. I wanted to help my patients address these concerns. While the videos can be helpful, they're a bit generic. They've worked for many of my patients, but it's important to customize them according to individual needs. If you're interested, we're starting a new session of guided yoga and meditation classes this Sunday, specifically designed for pregnant women. It could be a great way for you to get started in a safe, structured environment."

I felt a sense of relief wash over me. "That sounds perfect," I said. "I really trust your advice, and I've always felt that you've been attentive to my concerns. Knowing that I'll start with guidance, personalized specifically for pregnant women, puts my mind at ease. I'm actually really excited about this!" The doctor smiled warmly and reassured me, "Great! I'll make sure you have all the information and support you need to get started. Remember, it's all about keeping you and your baby healthy and happy."

I attended my first class on a Sunday a session dedicated to guided meditation specifically for pregnant women. The atmosphere was incredibly uplifting, filled with women at various stages of their pregnancies; some further along, others just like me, navigating this journey for the first time. It was a place brimming with understanding and shared experiences.

The structure of our weekly sessions was thoughtfully laid out: Yoga from Monday to Friday, a rest day on Saturday, and then meditation every Sunday. That particular Sunday session lasted for an hour and even extended an extra 15 minutes, but I didn't mind at all. It was, without exaggeration, one of the most meaningful days I'd experienced so far. I left feeling lighter, bursting with enthusiasm, and touched by a deep sense of positivity that resonated through every part of me.

As the weeks progressed, the daily yoga sessions became a ritual that I looked forward to. Each pose, each breath, brought subtle changes to my body, mind, and soul. Pregnancy is a transformative period you evolve in every conceivable way, mentally and physically. It's a time of heightened mindfulness, where your every action is infused with the intention of nurturing not just yourself but the new life growing inside you.

Pregnancy is undeniably a beautiful journey, but it's also punctuated with its fair share of challenges. There are days filled with pain, anxiety, and fear. Your mind sometimes becomes a battleground of random thoughts and mood swings. Despite these struggles, the support and guidance I found in these yoga and meditation sessions gave me strength. They reminded me that while pregnancy has its ups and downs, each step is a vital part of this incredible adventure.

Through this holistic approach, I learned to listen more intently to my body's needs and to connect more deeply with my baby. It became clear that by embracing both the physical and mental exercises, I was not only preparing myself for childbirth but also establishing foundations of well-being that would benefit both me and my child long after delivery.

As a working professional, I faced the relentless challenge of dealing with new physical pains every day sometimes it was my legs, other times my back, and frequently, debilitating headaches. This constant discomfort added to the stress of my already demanding life. Beyond my professional duties.

Balancing pregnancy with work was tough but doable. Meditation became my safe space, giving me mental peace and helping me manage my anxiety. Meditation became my sanctuary, bringing profound mental peace and helping me conquer my anxiety. Despite having little reason to worry, I found myself trapped in a cycle of overthinking.

Incorporating yoga into my routine was a game-changer. I remember a time when even a short five-minute walk was excruciating; the searing pain in my lower back and the weakness in my legs made such a simple activity feel like a challenge. However, with consistent practice, I began to notice a significant improvement. After a few weeks, I could walk for 20 minutes without discomfort, and eventually, I could manage a full hour of physical activity.I remember when a short five-minute walk was so painful that it felt impossible. My lower back hurt so much, and my legs felt weak. But with regular yoga, I started to feel better. After a few weeks, I could walk for 20 minutes without pain, and eventually, I could handle an hour of activity.

This journey taught me that being mentally fit is key to achieving anything. Knowing how we act, feel, and respond to others is important for keeping harmony in our relationships. For example, when I felt overwhelmed by work or family duties, I used mindfulness techniques to stay calm. Instead of reacting quickly to stress, I learned to take a moment, breathe, and respond calmly.

Yoga wasn't just about physical strength, though. It also helped me feel more connected to my body and more in tune with my feelings. This connection made it easier to notice when I was starting to feel stressed or anxious, so I could take steps to calm myself before those feelings got out of hand. For instance, if I felt a headache coming on, I would pause, take a few deep breaths, and stretch gently. Often, this was enough to stop the headache in its tracks.

Meditation, on the other hand, gave me a different kind of strength. It helped me quiet my mind and find peace amid the chaos. I started with just a few minutes a day, sitting quietly and focusing on my breath. Over time, I worked up to longer sessions. The more I meditated, the more I noticed a change in how I handled stress. I became less reactive and more thoughtful in my responses.

Whether dealing with family members or coworkers, being at peace inside makes a big difference. Meditation gave me that peace, helping me manage my responsibilities with a clear and focused mind. When I was calm, my interactions with others improved a lot. I became more patient with my baby, more supportive of my husband, and more effective at work. This inner peace created a positive atmosphere around me.

10. Financial Planning

The realization that a new life is on the way brings an overwhelming mix of emotions excitement, anticipation, and, of course, the weight of financial responsibility. When we discovered we were expecting, it wasn't part of our immediate plan, but we were thrilled nonetheless. My husband and I had always been diligent about budgeting and saving, and thankfully, both of us had stable and well-paying jobs. Still, the thought of adding a child to our lives required us to take a closer look at our finances and adapt to this new chapter.

For us, financial fitness wasn't just about having money in the bank; it was about being prepared for the future, understanding our priorities, and making choices that reflected our values as parents-to-be. To us, being financially fit meant creating a safety net, avoiding unnecessary debt, and ensuring we had the flexibility to provide for our child without sacrificing long-term goals like travel, education, or retirement. It wasn't about perfection or endless wealth it was about having the tools and mindset to handle the journey ahead confidently.

Our financial discussions began almost immediately after the initial euphoria settled. The thought of welcoming a baby brought warmth to our hearts but also a pragmatic awareness: babies come with their own set of expenses, and they add up quickly. One thing that worked in our favor was our habit of monthly financial check-ins. Every month, we'd sit together, sift through expenses, evaluate our savings, and map out upcoming financial goals. These discussions weren't always exciting it's hard to get enthusiastic about bills and spreadsheets but they gave us clarity and control. Now, with the arrival of our baby on the horizon, these meetings have become the backbone of our planning.

The first step was to break down the financial aspects into categories, starting with pre-birth costs. Regular doctor visits, ultrasounds, and prenatal vitamins quickly became routine expenses. Then came the hospital charges for delivery, which, depending on the type of delivery and hospital, could vary significantly. We researched these costs meticulously and chose a hospital that struck the right balance between quality and affordability. Beyond medical expenses, there were other pre-birth necessities that seemed small at first but added up quickly. Items like maternity clothing, a pregnancy pillow, and prenatal classes turned out to be more important than I initially thought.

As the pregnancy progressed, we began preparing for the baby's arrival. This was both exciting and overwhelming. The list of essentials seemed endless: a crib, mattress, baby clothes, diapers, feeding bottles, car seats, and strollers. Walking through baby stores was a mix of wonder and intimidation. Every item seemed to scream, "Buy me! The baby needs this!" But we had to remain practical. We approached these purchases methodically, focusing on what was truly necessary and safe. For instance, when buying a car seat, safety was non-negotiable. We spent hours reading reviews and comparing features before deciding. Similarly, for the crib, we avoided ornate designs and chose something simple yet sturdy.

One of the most helpful things we did during this time was to create a list of everything we'd need before the baby arrived. It gave us clarity and made the whole process feel less daunting. Here's what our list looked like:

For the Baby:

- A crib or bassinet
- Diapers (in multiple sizes) and wipes

- Baby clothes (newborn to 3 months)
- Baby blankets and swaddles
- Feeding supplies (bottles, breast pump, formula if needed)
- A car seat (essential for hospital discharge)
- A stroller
- Baby toiletries (baby-safe soap, shampoo, lotion)
- First-aid essentials (thermometer, nail clippers, etc.)

For the Parents:

- A hospital bag packed with essentials for both mom and dad
- Comfortable postpartum clothing
- Nursing supplies (if breastfeeding)
- Snacks and drinks for the hospital stay
- Important documents (insurance, ID, medical records)

For the Home:

- A clean, organized nursery or designated baby space
- Stocked pantry and freezer meals for those hectic first weeks

- Cleaning supplies (because things can get messy!)

Creating this list early gave us a sense of control. It helped us plan our purchases, prioritize what we needed first, and stick to our budget. We also spread out the expenses across several months, easing the financial burden and giving us time to make thoughtful decisions. We took advantage of sales and used gift cards.

While managing these immediate expenses, we also thought about the long-term picture. Babies don't just bring pre-birth costs; they come with a lifetime of needs pediatrician visits, vaccinations, baby food, clothes, and eventually, education. Being financially fit meant anticipating these future costs and building a contingency fund. This fund wasn't just for emergencies; it was for the "what if" scenarios complications during delivery, unexpected medical tests, or realizing we'd overlooked a key item. Having this cushion allowed us to approach the pregnancy with less anxiety.

We also made small lifestyle adjustments to accommodate these changes. Cutting back on dining out and impulse shopping freed up funds for baby-related costs. Surprisingly, these changes didn't feel like sacrifices. Instead, they brought us closer together as a couple. We'd cook meals at home, savoring these last few months of life as just the two of us before everything changed.

Another important aspect of our financial planning was making sure we have the right insurance coverage. Even though being financially fit isn't just about having insurance it's about being prepared for all the financial demands that come with parenthood, insurance covers a significant portion of not just medical expenses, but other costs, like those for baby essentials, childcare, and future education, must also be factored in. As to-be parents, financial fitness means striking a balance between meeting immediate needs and planning for the long term. Building an emergency fund can be a lifesaver, providing a safety net for unexpected costs. Adjusting your household budget to accommodate new expenses, such as diapers, baby food, and vaccinations, is another essential step.

In a world where expenses grow exponentially, ensuring financial preparedness is more important than ever especially when a baby is on the way. The joy of welcoming a new life is unmatched, but it also brings with it an undeniable surge in responsibilities. Among these, securing comprehensive health insurance stands out as a pillar of support. It's not just about mitigating medical costs; it's about accessing quality care, reducing financial stress, and making one of life's most significant transitions smoother.

For corporate employees, health insurance often comes as part of their employment benefits. However, simply having a policy isn't enough; understanding how to maximize it is crucial. Insurance plays a pivotal role in navigating the maternity journey, from regular check-ups to the unpredictable nature of childbirth. The ability to plan, prepare, and utilize these benefits can be the difference between a chaotic experience and one that allows you to focus on the well-being of your growing family.

One of the most valuable aspects of modern health insurance is the option for cashless services. For expecting parents, this feature can be a game-changer. Instead of worrying about arranging funds at the last minute, the hospital bills are settled directly by the insurance provider, making the process hassle-free. Cashless services allow you to focus entirely on the medical care required without the additional burden of financial logistics. The alternative non-cashless insurance requires you to pay the bills upfront and then claim reimbursement later. While this system offers similar coverage, the administrative workload, coupled with the need for detailed documentation, can add stress during an already intense time. When preparing for delivery, especially in cases where timing is unpredictable, opting for a cashless system wherever possible can simplify the experience significantly.

Selecting the hospital where your baby will be delivered is a deeply personal decision, but it should also align with your insurance policy. The emotional aspect of picking a place that feels welcoming and secure is vital, but so are practical considerations like the hospital's tie-ups with your insurance provider. Cashless hospitals streamline the entire process, from admission to discharge, ensuring minimal financial strain. Begin by verifying whether the hospital you're considering is part of your insurance network. It's equally important to visit the hospital beforehand. Familiarize yourself with the route, parking, and emergency services it's like rehearsing for the big day. A little preparation can save you precious time when every second counts.

When both partners are working and covered under separate corporate insurance plans, the potential benefits can be immense. However, effective coordination is key. Start by reviewing the maternity coverage offered by both policies, noting the limits, inclusions, and exclusions. Once you've assessed the options, prioritize the policy that offers the most comprehensive benefits.

For instance, if one policy covers a higher percentage of maternity costs or includes additional services such as neonatal care, it makes sense to designate this as the primary policy. The secondary policy can then be used for any expenses that exceed the primary policy's coverage. This approach maximizes the utility of both plans, ensuring that you minimize out-of-pocket expenses.

Informing your HR department about your intention to use maternity benefits is an essential step. Corporate policies often require pre-approval for maternity claims, so completing the necessary paperwork early on can save you from last-minute complications. Communicating with your insurer about expected delivery dates and required documentation ensures that everything is in place well before the critical moment.

By the time you enter the ninth month of pregnancy, the anticipation is palpable. It's also the time when thorough preparation can make a world of difference. Unexpected situations can arise, and being unprepared can lead to unnecessary stress. Start by updating your insurance details adding your spouse as a dependent if applicable and confirming that all records are accurate. This is also the time to gather all necessary documents. Create a folder with your insurance policy, ID proofs, medical reports, and pre-authorization forms. Having these ready means you won't waste precious time hunting for papers in an emergency. Inform your insurance provider or HR representative about the due date, giving them enough notice to ensure that approvals and processes are in place.

In my case, my husband's policy offered a higher coverage limit and, most importantly, a cashless facility at the hospital we had shortlisted for delivery. My policy, on the other hand, covered less and required us to pay upfront and then go through the process of reimbursement. It was clear that we should use his policy as the primary one and keep mine as a backup for any additional expenses.

The first step was ensuring that I was listed as a dependent under his policy. Thankfully, we had updated his insurance after our wedding, so we only needed to confirm the details with his HR department. His company's insurance representative walked us through the pre-authorization process, which gave us peace of mind knowing that everything was set well in advance.

On my end, I contacted my HR department to understand the steps for reimbursement. I made a checklist of documents I'd need hospital bills, reports, prescriptions, and receipts so we could keep everything organized right from the start.

When the time came, having everything ready made all the difference. At the hospital, we simply provided my husband's insurance details, and the cashless process was smooth and hassle-free. Later, I used my policy to claim reimbursement for some additional expenses. Because we had prepared and followed up promptly, the reimbursement process was straightforward and stress-free.

Key Points:

Welcoming a child into the world is a monumental change, one that reshapes every aspect of life, including finances. But with careful planning, open communication, and a willingness to adapt, it's a change that brings more joy than stress. While insurance is a financial tool, its real value lies in the peace of mind it offers. It allows you to focus on the joyous aspects of pregnancy and parenthood without being overshadowed by financial concerns. The key is to plan early, stay informed, and make thoughtful decisions.

From choosing the right hospital to coordinating dual policies and preparing for contingencies, insurance can transform what could be a stressful journey into a manageable and even enjoyable one. By understanding its nuances and leveraging its benefits, you can approach this life-changing chapter with confidence and clarity

The goal of insurance isn't just to save money it's to create a foundation of security, allowing you to give your growing family the care and attention they deserve. As you step into this new phase, let insurance be your silent partner, working behind the scenes to make every moment as smooth and memorable as possible.

Looking back, this phase of financial planning wasn't just about numbers and spreadsheets. It was about adapting to a new reality, making thoughtful choices, and prioritizing what truly mattered. Financial fitness as parents meant more than just managing money it was about creating a stable, nurturing foundation for our child and embracing the journey ahead.

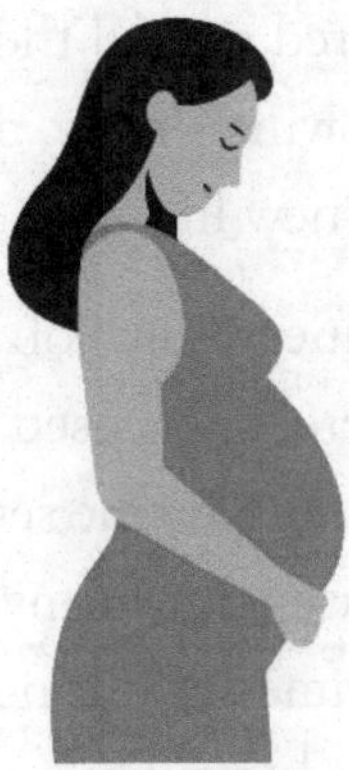

11.
The Third Trimester

The third trimester marked the beginning of a true battle. After the ease and joy of my second trimester, this final stretch brought new challenges that tested my physical and mental endurance. Everything had felt so balanced and fulfilling just a few months before, but now, with each passing day, I felt the weight of pregnancy in a very real way.

This trimester was where the true physical strains of pregnancy began to show up. My body had changed significantly: I had gained weight, and my belly was now prominently round, reflecting the baby's growth. Simple movements that I once took for granted sitting, standing, even lying down required careful thought and planning. I was no longer just "showing." Now, my entire body felt the demands of carrying a new life.

As a software engineer, my job involves long hours sitting in front of a screen, focused on solving problems and meeting deadlines. But by the seventh month, I began to experience an intense pain in my tailbone that started mildly in my second trimester but now felt all-consuming. It was as if a constant, heavy pressure bore down on my lower back and tailbone, making it unbearable to sit for more than a few minutes at a time. I tried every possible solution tailbone cushions, posture-support pillows, standing breaks but nothing seemed to bring lasting relief. The physical toll began to affect my focus and productivity, draining me both mentally and emotionally.

What made it even harder was knowing that during pregnancy, pain management options are limited. The usual remedies like painkillers or muscle relaxants weren't safe choices, as they could potentially affect the baby's development. So, I had to face the reality that this pain would be part of my daily life until the baby arrived. Accepting this was tough, especially as the discomfort grew worse over time. As my belly continued to expand, the pain intensified, adding a sense of helplessness that was difficult to shake.

Nights, which I once looked forward to as a time to recharge, became an entirely different struggle. Sleep was elusive; I would lie awake, my mind tired but my body unable to rest. I was always too hot, tossing and turning to find a comfortable position. My husband, who was as supportive as he could be, would often be shivering beside me while I was uncomfortably warm. My body seemed determined to defy the need for rest, and each night became a test of patience and endurance.

What's more, each day seemed to bring a new challenge. One day it would be swelling in my feet and hands; the next, it would be difficulty breathing or simply feeling too exhausted to focus on anything. It was as if my body was constantly adapting to the demands of this final stretch, but every adaptation came with its own discomfort. Emotionally, I felt like I was in a tug-of-war with myself. I wanted to be productive at work and to contribute to my team, but my body was sending clear signals that it needed a break.

Balancing work became an intense, sometimes overwhelming challenge in the third trimester, as if my mind and body were in constant negotiation. For me, work wasn't just a job; it was a comforting escape, a space where I could focus my energy and, for a few hours, feel grounded in familiar routines. Dedicating myself to projects and deadlines allowed me to temporarily set aside the aches and struggles of pregnancy. With each task, I felt a sense of accomplishment that boosted my spirit and made me feel more like myself. Work became my safe haven, a place where I could find respite in productivity, something tangible to hold onto as my body carried me through this transformative journey.

Yet, not all days cooperated with my ambitions. I would start the day with goals, motivated to make progress, only to realize that my body had its own plans. There were days when I felt capable and energized, able to dive into tasks and keep up with my usual pace. But more often than not, the physical discomforts soreness, backaches, and the relentless weight of the growing baby made sitting at my desk a struggle. I'd find myself shifting in my chair, adjusting my position every few minutes, and even then, the discomfort lingered. Just sitting through meetings or focusing for prolonged periods felt like an accomplishment.

On those harder days, when my energy was low and pain made even simple tasks feel exhausting, I couldn't help but feel frustrated. My usual enthusiasm for work was replaced by a deep need to rest. Long hours left me feeling drained and irritable, yearning to shut down my laptop, close my eyes, and simply sleep. The emotional toll weighed heavily, too; it was hard to accept that my body's limitations were dictating my productivity. There was a constant push and pull between wanting to excel in my role and accepting the reality that my body needed rest more than it needed to check items off a to-do list.

Eventually, I had to adjust my expectations of what a successful day looked like. Instead of measuring my worth by the number of tasks completed, I learned to appreciate small victories. If I could finish a small task, attend a meeting, or make meaningful progress on a project, it was a win. Letting go of my usual benchmarks for productivity was tough, especially as someone who takes pride in a job well done and finds satisfaction in reaching goals. But pregnancy was teaching me new dimensions of patience, resilience, and adaptability. Every task completed was a testament to my strength, a reminder that I was balancing two monumental roles bringing new life into the world and continuing to contribute to my work.

Through this journey, I began to see work in a new light, as both a comforting retreat and, at times, a daunting challenge. On good days, it gave me a focus that allowed me to forget the discomfort for a while, bringing back a sense of routine and normalcy when everything else felt in flux. It felt like a place where I could still be me, not just someone preparing to become a mother. But there were other days when work demanded an energy my body simply couldn't give. On those days, it reminded me that rest wasn't a weakness but a necessity, and I had to learn to accept that, even if it meant leaving tasks unfinished.

I realized, little by little, that success didn't have to mean crossing off every item on my to-do list. Some days, just showing up and giving what I could was enough. This phase of pregnancy taught me that strength isn't always loud or visible; sometimes, it's in the quiet act of doing your best even if that means slowing down, listening to what your body needs, and finding peace in simply being present, one day at a time.

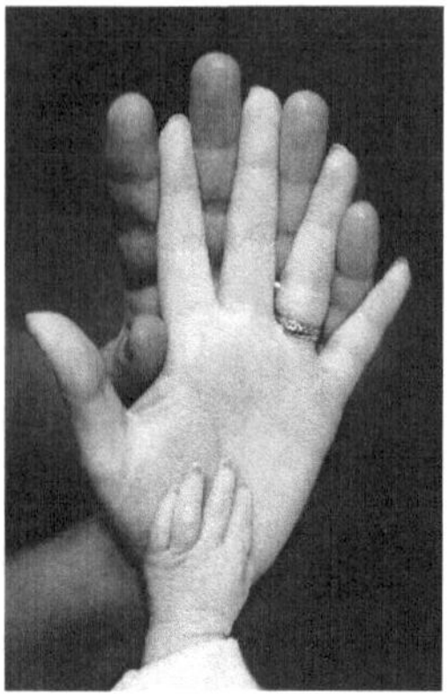

12.
The Labor Day

The Day That Came Too Soon...

The labor day holds a special place in this journey a day filled with unexpected twists, emotions, and realizations that forever changed my life. It's a story I want to tell with all its rawness and honesty because it's not just about the birth of a child, but the birth of a mother.

When I envisioned the day I would go into labor, I had a plan. I had imagined every detail meticulously, from staying calm to making it to the hospital right on schedule. But as life often teaches us, some moments are beyond planning.

The day didn't unfold the way I had anticipated. In fact, it came earlier 15 days earlier to be precise. And that's where the story begins.

Funny how the universe works I always said I wanted to work until the very last day of my pregnancy, and it seems the universe was listening.

For weeks, friends, colleagues, and even family urged me to take my maternity leave early, to rest and prepare for the big day. But something inside me wasn't convinced. I wanted to keep going, to stay connected to my work routine until the very end.

The signs started two days after a routine checkup with my doctor. During that visit, she casually mentioned, "There's a chance you may deliver about a week early, so stay alert. Also, start doing Malasana and Butterfly poses twice a day it'll help with the process." My husband and I nodded, taking her advice in stride, but we didn't overthink it. Back home, we shared the update with our family, which naturally sparked a lively debate.

"Doctors always say these things to make you cautious," everyone remarked. "You'll probably go the full 40 weeks. Don't worry."

We took these comments lightly, brushing them off with a casual we'll see what happens. But the nights that followed were anything but normal for me. I couldn't sleep. I felt restless, unable to find a comfortable position no matter how hard I tried. The frequent trips to the bathroom were relentless. By the second night, I was utterly drained.

When I shared this with my family, they dismissed it as typical for the final stretch of pregnancy. "It's normal," they said. "The last days are always the hardest. Hang in there!" Their reassurances were kind but did little to ease my discomfort.

That morning, as my husband prepared for work, he paused. "Should I stay home today? You don't seem well," he asked, his eyes filled with concern.

"No, I'm fine," I replied, trying to sound convincing. "Go to the office. If I need you, I'll call."

But his instincts were stronger than my words. He decided to work from home, convincing his manager with a quick conversation. Looking back, I'm grateful he did.

By noon, I was logged into work, attending meetings, and even wrapping up my tasks. I had mentioned to my team earlier that there was a possibility of an early delivery. My manager, ever understanding, said, "Wrap up what you can, but don't stress yourself. This is your second-last day focus on resting."

Taking her advice to heart, I worked steadily, tying up loose ends, giving final handovers, and ensuring my responsibilities were in order. By 4 PM, I was done or so I thought. Suddenly, a wave of exhaustion hit me. There was a dull ache in my lower abdomen, growing stronger by the minute.

"Take a break," my husband suggested. "Rest for a bit, then get back to it if you feel better."

I agreed and lay down, hoping to recharge. But the discomfort didn't fade. I forced myself to finish one last meeting, closed my laptop, and officially called it a day.

Coincidentally, my sister-in-law visited that evening to check on me. "You don't look too great," she said casually, adding with a smile, "I think the baby's coming soon."

Her words didn't alarm me then, but now they feel prophetic. We had tea and chatted briefly, but I couldn't sit with them for long. The discomfort was intensifying. I excused myself, returning to bed, only to find myself making repeated trips to the bathroom. Every five minutes, it seemed, I had to go. It was exhausting and frustrating.

And then, I noticed it a pinkish discharge, heavier than what I'd seen earlier that morning. My heart skipped a beat. It wasn't just the discharge; it was accompanied by period-like cramps in my abdomen and a persistent ache in my lower back.

This wasn't normal. Something was happening. My mind raced as I tried to process what was unfolding. The moment I had been waiting for anxious about, excited for, and nervous about was finally here.

The signs were there, but I was hesitant. Should I tell my family about what I was experiencing? Should I wait it out? The uncertainty loomed large as I quietly retreated to my room, my mind racing with questions and doubts.

Unable to shake off the anxious thoughts, I turned to Google, my ever-reliable companion during moments of doubt. I searched for "symptoms of labor pain" and was greeted with a list of signs:

- Period-like cramps in the lower abdomen
- Mucus discharge
- Nesting instincts

There were others, but these three caught my attention they aligned perfectly with what I was feeling. Anxiety gripped me. Was this it? Was my baby on its way?

Taking a deep breath, I walked out to the dining hall, trying to keep my composure. I shared my concerns with my sister-in-law, mentioning the heavy pinkish discharge I had noticed. She listened carefully and immediately advised, "Contact your doctor right away."

I hesitated for a moment but then sent pictures and a brief description of my symptoms to my doctor. Her response was swift and clear: "*Come to the hospital immediately and get admitted. These are labor signs. By tonight, you might experience intense labor pains, which could create a panic situation. It's better to be here early.*"

Her words hit me like a wave. It was happening, and it was happening now. Still, doubt lingered. What if this wasn't real labor? To ensure we were making the right decision, my sister-in-law reached out to a gynecologist she trusted, explaining my situation and symptoms. To our reassurance, the second opinion aligned with the first. It solidified our confidence to act without hesitation.

We decided to head to the hospital after dinner, though I could barely eat a thing. My mind was spinning. The rapid pace of events was overwhelming. I couldn't help but think about work *Had I pushed the code before closing my laptop? Did I leave any loose ends?*

I voiced these thoughts to my husband, who gently but firmly reassured me, "It's normal to feel this way, but right now, work is the least of your concerns. Inform your team while we're on our way to the hospital and focus on yourself. Pack your essentials. Whatever's missing, I'll get it by morning."

His calm demeanor grounded me. I packed our hospital bag, double-checked everything I might need for the hospital, and changed into comfortable clothes. Meanwhile, my husband finalized the essentials we had discussed earlier.

As we drove to the hospital, I composed a message to my manager and team members, informing them about my early labor and the immediate need to step away from work. In that moment, a profound sense of gratitude filled me as I reflected on the support I had received from my workplace. My manager, in particular, had gone above and beyond to ensure my workload was manageable during the third trimester. They had been incredibly thoughtful, assigning me tasks that were less critical and steering clear of any high-pressure deadlines or urgent projects.

This wasn't just a managerial decision; it was a gesture of genuine care and understanding. They recognized my dedication and knew I was someone who would always strive to deliver my best, even when the circumstances might not allow it. By easing my responsibilities during those final weeks, they allowed me to focus on my health and prepare mentally and emotionally for the arrival of my baby.

Looking back, this proactive approach made a world of difference. It wasn’t just about reducing stress it was about feeling seen and supported as an employee and as a soon-to-be mother. Their empathy and foresight created a space where I could transition smoothly, knowing that everything at work was under control and my team had my back. It was a rare and invaluable kind of support, one that I’ll always carry with immense appreciation.

When we arrived at the hospital, everything unfolded smoothly, almost like clockwork. The admission process, which could have been overwhelming and chaotic in such a high-stress situation, was surprisingly calm. This sense of order was the result of our careful planning. Weeks before the big day, my husband and I had done a mock drill something we joked about at the time but quickly became one of the smartest decisions we'd made. We had familiarized ourselves with every aspect of the hospital, from the parking lot to the emergency ward. We knew exactly where to park, the quickest route to get to the ward, and what to expect when we walked through the doors. We even discussed what paperwork we might need and how to navigate the hospital's layout. At that moment, all that preparation paid off. Instead of scrambling, we felt confident and calm. It was like a rehearsal that ensured we weren't caught off guard by any unexpected details. The chaos that can so easily erupt in such a stressful moment was completely absent, and we were able to focus on what really mattered getting ready for the next step in this life-changing journey.

The moment we entered the emergency ward, things picked up pace quickly. Nurses and doctors took over, checking my vitals and monitoring the baby's heart rate closely. The doctor, her expression steady but kind, confirmed what I had already suspected, "You're in labor. By tonight, it's going to get more intense. We'll induce labor to help move things along." Her words were direct, but they didn't overwhelm me. I felt a sense of certainty that I was where I needed to be.

While I was prepped for what was to come, my husband handled the paperwork and made sure everything was in order. The process felt surreal, like watching everything unfold in slow motion. But as chaotic as it felt in some ways, there was also a quiet reassurance this was the path we'd been preparing for, and everything was falling into place.

By the time we moved to the room later that night, the pain was stronger, and I could feel my body adjusting to the reality of labor. It wasn't easy. Every contraction felt like a tight knot being pulled in my abdomen, and I braced myself for the next wave. But through it all, having my husband and sister-in-law by my side made all the difference. They were my support system, keeping the mood light, offering words of comfort, and reminding me that I wasn't alone. It was the kind of calm I needed in the storm of labor.

After nearly 20 hours of labor, which felt like an endless stretch of time, I finally held my daughter for the first time. The moment I held her in my arms, everything changed. All the pain, the worry, the anxiety everything faded into the background. It was like none of it mattered anymore. The sleepless nights, the preparation, the uncertainty all of it was worth it. This little life, so precious and fragile, made every second of labor feel like a distant memory.

Looking back, that day taught me more than just the physical journey of childbirth. It was a lesson in patience, resilience, and the importance of being prepared not just for the practical side of things, but for the emotional rollercoaster that came with it. Labor didn't go as planned, but it turned out to be exactly what I needed. The support of my husband , the reassurance of my sister-in-law, the encouragement from my workplace, and the collective care of my family and in-laws helped me handle the chaos. When it was all over, I realized that sometimes, it's these unexpected moments and the people who rally around us that shape us the most.

Note for Husband

Dear Husband,

As we journey through this significant phase of our lives, I want to take a moment to thank you for all the efforts you make to keep this pregnancy journey beautiful. This is a transformative time for both of us, filled with moments that will be etched in our hearts forever. From the moment we found out that we were not just partners but soon-to-be parents, our lives changed in ways we couldn't have imagined. I remember the look on your face when we heard our baby's heartbeat for the first time it was a moment of pure magic, a sound that seemed to promise so much joy and possibility. I could see the awe in your eyes, and it made me realize how much this journey meant to both of us.

As my body began to change, showing signs of the life growing within me, you were there every step of the way, witnessing the miracle . I remember when you first felt the movements of our baby, your hand gently resting on my belly, your face lighting up with wonder and excitement. Those little kicks were like a secret language between us and our baby, a reminder of the beautiful journey we were on together.

Watching my body transform wasn't always easy, but you never failed to remind me of the beauty in it. Your words of encouragement and your unwavering support gave me strength and confidence when I needed it most. You made me feel cherished and loved, and your presence was a constant source of comfort and reassurance.

These moments the first flutter of life, the anticipation of holding our child, and the quiet moments of reflection as we prepared for parenthood are irreplaceable. They are memories we will carry with us forever, etched into the fabric of our lives. Each moment is unique and special, reminding us of the profound connection we share.

I want you to know that a woman never forgets how she was treated during her pregnancy. The kindness,care, patience, and understanding you have shown me during this time have not gone unnoticed. Your efforts to make this journey beautiful and meaningful have strengthened our bond and deepened our love.As we continue on this path, let's cherish these little moments together the ones that make us laugh, the ones that bring tears of joy, and the ones that remind us of the incredible life we are creating. Let's celebrate the changes, embrace the challenges, and hold onto the love that brought us here.

Thank you, dear husband, for being my partner, my rock, and my greatest supporter. Thank you for making this pregnancy journey a beautiful journey that we share, hand in hand, heart to heart.

With all my love,
Aditi <3

Note for Family

Do you know what a true blessing is? A supportive family. During the beautiful yet challenging journey of pregnancy, having the unwavering support of my family felt like a gift beyond words. It's not just about becoming parents a new life brings a wave of joy that touches everyone in the family. I am deeply thankful to my entire family and in-laws for their love and care. It's the small, heartfelt gestures that truly made all the difference.

Each person played their role in their own special way, but I want to express my heartfelt gratitude to a few extraordinary people who stood by me when I needed them the most. To my sisters-in-law Neerja di, Seema di, and Rinki di , my mother-in-law, my mother, and my sister Vaishnavi: without you, I don't know how I would have made it through this journey.

Neerja Di: You have been my rock, always knowing exactly what I needed, often before I even realized it myself. Your instincts were incredible, and your thoughtful tips and recipes, customized to each stage of my pregnancy, were lifesavers. You have been the elder sister I always wished for, offering love, wisdom, and constant support. I am so grateful for your presence and guidance.

Seema Di and Rinki Di: Even though you both live miles away, you found ways to make me feel supported and connected. Our video calls were more than just conversations; they were moments of reassurance. Seema Di, as the newest mother in the family, your stories, advice, and practical tips helped me overcome the uncertainties with grace and insight. You kept me prepared and grounded, making this journey less daunting. Having not one, but three amazing elder sisters to shower me and my baby with love has been such a blessing.

My Mother: There are no words to truly capture what you mean to me. You are my everything. Post-pregnancy, when my body felt weak and exhausted, you were my strength. You cared for me in ways only a mother can, helping me rebuild my energy and spirit. Those first 15 days were some of the toughest, but your unwavering presence made them manageable. You showed me that it's not just the birth of a baby, but the birth of a mother. I couldn't have done it without you.

My Mother-in-Law: Your support was instrumental in helping me balance recovery and daily life. You ensured I followed my diet and took my meals on time, which played a big role in my routine and well-being. Your discipline and care allowed me to focus on myself and my baby, knowing everything else was taken care of. I am so grateful for your love and attention during this time.

Vaishnavi, My Sister: You are my lifeline. Pregnancy brought a rollercoaster of emotions, and you handled every moment with grace. Whether I was elated, anxious, or frustrated, you were always there to listen and support me. Even though you are younger than me, your maturity and calmness amazed me. I don't know how I would have managed without you. You're my anchor, and I can't thank you enough.

To my father, father-in-law, my sister Amrita, and every other family member who was part of this journey: thank you from the bottom of my heart. Your love and encouragement made this time in my life so much more meaningful.

This experience has shown me that family is not just about being related by blood. It's about the connections we build, the support we give, and the love we share. Together, we welcomed a new life into this world, and for that, I will always be grateful.